To,

Dear Lion Kanta ji,

Wishing you abundance of good
health, wealth, love, luck, joy
and peace in life forever!!

Love,
Mandvi
June 27, 2024

COPYRIGHT & DISCLAIMER:

© MANDVI GUPTA

1st Edition

Published & Distributed by Delta Publication

What we think determines what happens to us,
so if we want to change our lives,
we need to stretch our minds.

- Wayne Dyer

This book is dedicated to the
Power of the Universe embodied
in Human Mind,
waiting to be unleashed.

Table of Contents

FOREWORD

In today's fast-paced and demanding world, it has become increasingly important to prioritize our mental and emotional well-being. The power of positive thinking and self-affirmation has been widely acknowledged as a transformative tool for achieving personal growth and happiness. It is my privilege to introduce this insightful book about affirmations, a profound guide that will undoubtedly inspire and empower readers on their journey towards self-discovery and self-empowerment.

In this handy book, "Everything About Affirmations," the author emphasizes the profound impact that affirmations can have on our mindset, emotions, and actions. With insights garnered from extensive research, personal experiences, and the testimonies of clients, this book serves as a comprehensive guide to understanding the extraordinary power of the subconscious mind through affirmations.

This powerful book will help you discover a treasure trove of affirmations tailored to various aspects of life, including self-esteem, abundance, healing, love, and inner peace. Each affirmation is like a compass, guiding you towards your true potential and reminding you of your inherent worthiness.

I congratulate Mandvi for her dedication, wisdom, and heartfelt commitment to sharing the transformative power of affirmations. It is my sincere belief that this book will become a trusted companion on your quest for personal fulfillment and joy. It will remind you that you possess the power to rewrite your story, to reclaim your inner strength, and to create a life filled with purpose and meaning. By incorporating affirmations into your daily life, you will cultivate a mindset of positivity, resilience, and abundance.

So, dear reader, I invite you to open your heart and mind to the power of affirmations and allow them to illuminate your path towards a life of abundance, fulfillment, and unwavering belief in your own infinite potential.

With heartfelt blessings,

Bharti Chauhan

TED India- Coach & Principal partner,
Founder-Humming together,
Chairperson Success Torch Pvt. Ltd.
Program leader /leadership coach Iron Lady/
Director India Coaching Federation

ACKNOWLEDGEMENT

First and foremost, I want to thank the incredible women who shaped me into the person I am today: Ma and my loving sisters. You have been my biggest source of strength and inspiration throughout my life. Your unwavering love, support, and guidance have encouraged me to dream high and grow beyond my own expectations, I am eternally grateful.

Gratitude to my father, who has taught me patience and the concept of "attachment with detachment".

I am indebted to Jija ji, who has taught me to live life with a larger purpose. His generosity, support, and encouragement propel me to achieve higher goals in my life. I am truly blessed to have you as a guide in my life.

Heartfelt gratitude to my husband, who helped me push my limits and create the foundation for unlimited success. I extend my love and gratitude to my son, who has been my youngest cheerleader, for his support and for the title of this book.

I am grateful to my whole family, Soka-family, friends, colleagues, and clients, whose unwavering support and encouragement have fueled my passion for motivating others. Your love and belief in my abilities have given me the strength to overcome any obstacles that block my way. Many thanks to Hema for being the most committed believer in my guidance and practicing it to achieve numerous victories in her life. Thank you for believing in me. This dedication is a humble acknowledgement of the invaluable role you all play in my life.

I am grateful to my mentor, Bharti ma'am, for always encouraging me and writing the foreword to this book.

Sincere gratitude to the readers who have picked up this book. Your interest in my work means the world to me, and I hope the ideas and advice within these pages prove valuable in your journey toward self-improvement.

Lastly, I'd like to acknowledge the countless authors and mentors' whose work has inspired me to move forward in life despite challenges. Your wisdom has been a guiding light, and I am honored to be able to contribute to society.

This book is dedicated to all of you who have shaped my life, supported my dreams, and made me a better person. Without your love, guidance, and companionship, this journey would not have been possible.

Deepest gratitude from the depths of my heart,

Mandvi

INTRODUCTION

"The mind is everything. What you think you become."

- Buddha

In a world filled with constant noise and distractions, finding inner peace and self-assurance can often feel like an insurmountable challenge. In an environment that often tests your limits, challenges your beliefs, and subjects you to constant waves of doubt and uncertainty, affirmation stands as a beacon of hope, a guiding light that empowers you to rewrite your own golden story of victory.

It is a practice as ancient as the human spirit itself, harnessed by sages, philosophers, and visionaries throughout history to awaken humans' inner potential and reshape their external realities. In today's time, you all strive for happiness, success, and a sense of purpose. Sometimes doubts and negativity can suppress your dreams. In these critical moments, the practice of affirmation emerges as a powerful tool that can help you win over any challenge in life. As per the law of attraction, your physical reality (outer world) is a reflection of your inner world. Affirmations help us to transform your inner self, thus changing its reflection in the outer world (physical reality).

In this book, "Everything About Affirmations," you delve deep into the world of affirmations. This book is your comprehensive guide to understanding, harnessing, and mastering the art of affirmation. This book covers information about manifesting a life of your dreams by utilizing the power of affirmations positively.

1

Definition of affirmation from the Oxford Advanced Learner's Dictionary:

affirmation *noun*

/ˌæfəˈmeɪʃn/

/ˌæfərˈmeɪʃn/

(formal)

> [uncountable, countable] a definite or public statement that something is true or that you support something strongly.
>
> *website link -*
> *https://www.oxfordlearnersdictionaries.com/definition/e nglish/affirmation#:~:text=%2F%CB%8C%C3%A6f%C9% 99r%CB%88me%C9%AA%CA%83n%2F,support%20somet hing%20strongly%20synonym%20confirmation*

In simpler words, affirmation means to accept as true/ to agree/ to give consent to. As per this book, affirmations are the way to give your consent to the idea that you want to manifest or create in your life.

The power of affirmation is essentially the infinite potential that lies within our own lives. By using the tools explained further in this book, you can transform your life and claim the abundance lying within, waiting to be unlocked. This book will serve as a guide, providing the knowledge, tools, and inspiration needed to tap into that power and transform your life from within. Whether you are seeking to attract wealth and luxury, boost confidence, attract abundance, improve relationships, or find inner peace, affirmations can be your best companion towards achieving a brighter and more fulfilling future.

This book is a perfect comprehensive handbook for all, whether you are a beginner looking to incorporate affirmations into your life or someone experienced seeking to further polish your affirmation practice. This book lists customized affirmations in a very simple language that can be used to transform all areas of life, such as self-esteem, relationships, career, health, wealth, and spirituality, etc.

Prepare yourself to claim the universe through self-discovery, growth, and transformation. Through the pages of "Everything About Affirmations", you'll unlock the secrets to harnessing the power of positive thinking and thus shaping your destiny.

Disclaimer: It's important to note that while positive affirmations can be a valuable tool, they are not a substitute for professional help when dealing with severe issues. In such cases, it's essential to seek the guidance of a qualified professional. Additionally, the effectiveness of positive affirmations may vary from person to person, and it's essential to use them consistently and believe in their potential to bring about positive change.

CHAPTER-1
WHAT ARE AFFIRMATIONS?

*"Whatever we plant in our subconscious mind and nourish
with repetition and emotion will one day become a reality."*

- Earl Nightingale

The human mind is divided into two parts: Conscious mind and Subconscious mind, which play distinct roles in creating thoughts, feelings, behaviors, and outcomes in human life. Both the conscious and subconscious minds work together to shape your overall mental processes and physical realities. While the conscious mind is the rational, analytical, and critical thinking part. The subconscious mind stores beliefs, creativity, intuitions, habits, etc. that greatly influence our thoughts and behaviors. The conscious and subconscious mind work in tandem, with the subconscious mind contributing to 95% of our physical and mental responses. Your thoughts are nothing but the constant inner dialog running through your mind. Since the subconscious mind is active 24/7, whatever thoughts are repeated in the mind consciously become reality. Affirmations can be used to reprogram the subconscious mind and promote positive thinking and self-belief. By repeating affirmations regularly, you can reinforce positive beliefs, remove negative thoughts and self-doubt, and manifest desired outcomes.

Whatever statement you think, hear, speak, read, or write about life is an affirmation. Whatever you experience with your five senses—taste, smell, hearing, touch, and vision—becomes an affirmation when you experience the emotions are associated with it. You can use the power of positive affirmations to

4

transform your "current reality" into "desired reality". While using the power of affirmations, you constantly feed your subconscious mind with positive and empowering thoughts related to your goals/ desired reality. This in turn helps in creating reality through the energy and vibrations of your thoughts and emotions that flow across the entire universe through your physical body.

Affirmations can be used in all areas of life that affect our mental and physical well-being. You can manifest abundance of Health, Wealth, Relationships, Love, Success, Peace, Hope, Courage, and Career in your life by using the immense power of affirmations. This also helps in improving self-esteem, overcoming fears and anxieties, achieving goals, and fostering inner peace and happiness.

They can be written down, repeated out loud, or even visualized in order to make them more effective. It is important to consistently practice affirmations and have faith in their power to experience their full benefits.

By consciously choosing positive thoughts and repeating those affirmations, we can make a shift from a *"scarcity mindset"* to *"Abundance Mindset"* and attract desired positive experiences in our lives.

CHAPTER-2
WHO SHOULD AFFIRM?

"I choose to make the rest of my life the best of my life."

- Louise Hay

Affirmations can benefit anyone who wants to cultivate a positive mindset, improve self-belief, overcome negative thoughts, break through the cycle of negativity and procrastination, and achieve their goals. There are no specific limitations or restrictions on who can use affirmations; people of any age can unleash the power of affirmation. Whether you are struggling with low self-esteem, facing challenges in your personal or professional life, or simply seeking to enhance your overall well-being, affirmations can be a powerful tool for personal growth and transformation.

Affirmations can be particularly helpful for individuals who are ready to take action with faith in the infinite potential possessed within their lives. It is a tool for you to cultivate an abundant mindset arising from the faith that your life is filled with transformative power similar to the universe and you are worthy of all the positive experiences in life. Affirmations can also be useful for individuals who are working towards specific goals or aspirations, as they can help build confidence, maintain focus, and attract opportunities and success.

Ultimately, affirmations are a tool that anyone can utilize to fulfill their dreams. They can be adapted and personalized to suit individual needs, making them accessible and beneficial to people from all walks of life.

In short, anyone who is open to exploring the power of positive thinking and willing to incorporate affirmations into their daily routine can benefit from them. Whether you are a student, a professional, a parent, a homemaker, an entrepreneur, a senior citizen, or anyone seeking personal improvement, affirmations have the potential to positively impact your life. Each one of us possesses the power that lies within the whole universe; thus, each one of us is capable of creating our own destiny by using this wonderful tool of affirmations.

CHAPTER-3
WHY SHOULD YOU AFFIRM?

"Whatever your mind can conceive and believe, it can achieve."

- Napoleon Hill

If you are not satisfied with your current life condition in any area of your life and want to transform it into a different desired reality, then you should use this power existing in your life only. Several other benefits of incorporating affirmations into your life are:

1. Overcome limiting beliefs: Affirmations can help overcome limiting beliefs that may be holding you back in various aspects of life. By consciously replacing negative, self-defeating thoughts with positive affirmations, you can empower yourself to break free from self-imposed limitations and tap into your true potential.

2. Cultivate an abundance mindset: Affirmations can help cultivate a positive mindset by replacing negative thoughts and beliefs with positive ones. Through perseverance, you train your subconscious mind to focus on the positive aspects of life, leading to a more optimistic and uplifting outlook on life.

Affirmations works on the principles of the law of attraction, which suggests that positive thoughts and beliefs can attract positive experiences and outcomes into your life. By affirming abundance, success, and prosperity, you align your energy with those positive experiences, thus manifesting the same in your life.

3. Goal achievement: Affirmations can serve as powerful tools for goal achievement. This helps in finding the purpose and goals you want to achieve in life. Then, by affirming specific goals and visualizing their attainment, you program your subconscious mind to work towards those goals and attract opportunities and resources that align with your desires.

4. Self-belief and confidence: Affirmations can boost self-belief and confidence by reinforcing positive self-perception. By regularly affirming positive qualities and abilities, you build a strong foundation of self-confidence, which can help you take appropriate actions, overcome obstacles, and achieve your goals.

5. Increased motivation and productivity: Regular affirmations can provide a motivational boost and enhance productivity. By affirming your abilities, motivation, and focus, you can overcome procrastination, stay on track with your goals, and approach tasks with a positive and determined mindset.

6. Stress reduction and mental well-being: By incorporating affirmations into your daily routine, you can create a positive shift in your thoughts and actions, leading to personal growth, success, and a greater sense of fulfillment. Overall, affirmations can transform your mental state from "Victim to Victor". It empowers you to take actions in positive directions. In the event of a challenge, instead of thinking, "Why me"? You feel empowered to transform it into a victory. This helps to reduce stress and improve overall mental well-being by promoting self-care and self-compassion, fostering a healthier relationship with yourself, and reducing negative self-talk.

CHAPTER-4
WHEN SHOULD YOU AFFIRM?

There is no generic answer to when you should affirm; it largely depends on your personal preference and schedule. It is important to maintain consistency, discipline, and faith. It is preferable to do the affirmations daily at the same time of the day. The best time to do affirmations is just after waking up and before falling asleep. These are the ideal times to do your affirmations, as in these moments you are in the theta state of sleep. In this state, our conscious mind is not fully activated, thus giving more power to the subconscious mind. This reduces the resistance created by the logical and analytical conscious mind, thus expediting the manifestation of affirmations.

However, here are a few suggestions to incorporate it into your daily routine, you can choose the one that suits you the most as per your schedule:

1. Morning routine: Many people find it beneficial to start their day with affirmations. By affirming positive statements in the morning, you set the tone for the day ahead and establish a positive mindset. You can incorporate affirmations into your morning routine, whether it's hearing them while getting ready, writing them in a journal, through meditation or visualization, or simply by repeating them out loud or silently to yourself.

2. Before challenging situations: Affirmations can be especially helpful when facing challenging situations in life. By affirming your confidence, abilities, and positive outcomes. You can boost your self-belief and calm your nerves to attract desired results.

3. Throughout the day: You can also incorporate affirmations into your daily routine by repeating them at various times throughout the day. For example, you can have a list of affirmations on your phone or written on sticky notes and refer to them during breaks or downtime. You can even phrase your passwords for various websites/logins based on your affirmations. So, every time you type it, you affirm it. This helps to reinforce positive thinking and maintain a positive mindset throughout the day.

4. Before bedtime: Affirmations can also be used as part of your nighttime routine. By affirming positive thoughts and beliefs before sleep, you program your subconscious mind during the night, potentially leading to positive changes and manifestations. This helps promote relaxation, a sense of calm, and a peaceful state of mind before sleep.

Ultimately, the key is consistency and finding a routine that works for you. Experiment with different times of the day and observe how you feel and the impact it has on your mindset. It is important to choose a time when you can focus and give your full attention to the affirmations.

CHAPTER-5
HOW SHOULD YOU AFFIRM?

मनसयक वचसयक कममणयक महातमनामा

Manas Ekam Vachas Ekam, Karman Ekam Mahatmanam.

(This Sanskrit verse emphasizes that high-spirited individuals are those who have perfect harmony in their thoughts, words, and deeds)

This is the most crucial aspect of affirmation, as it requires clarity of your goals and understanding of your limiting beliefs about them. Once you decide to use this powerful tool in your life, you first need to determine which category you belong to:

1. Category 1: I don't know about my goals, but I certainly want to improve the quality of my life.

2. Category 2: I know my goals, but I don't know my limiting beliefs around them.

3. Category 3: I know my goals, and I know my limiting beliefs around them.

1. **Category 1- "I don't know about my goals, but I certainly want to improve the quality of my life":**

Congratulations to you! as you are choosing a path of growth in your life, and you want to improve the quality of your life. When you are not sure about specific goals at the moment, then reflecting on the following questions will help you assess your areas of improvement and define your specific goals:

Area of life	How satisfied are you with your current situation? (Rate on a scale of 1-10)	If the score is less than 7, then what reality do you want to create?
Career: Your professional ambitions and goals.		
Finances: Goals related to income, savings, and financial security.		
Health and Fitness: Goals related to physical and mental health.		
Personal Growth: Goals for learning and self-improvement.		
Relationships: Goals for building and maintaining meaningful connections with yourself and others around you.		
Spirituality: Goals related to fulfilling your purpose and giving back to the world through your interests and passions.		

Answers to the last column will give you clarity about your goals for affirmations. Once you are clear about your goals, follow the guidelines given for Category 2 and 3. Always select affirmations that are aligned with your goals and resonate with you. Below examples explain how to use the above questionnaire to get the insight about goals:

Example-1: If you are not satisfied with your relationship with any family member, then rating in "Relationships" area will be less than 7 and if your goal is to have an improved relationship, then you can work on "Affirmations for Family" (as per "List of Affirmations" at pg. 23.

Example-2: If you are not satisfied with income, then rating in "Finances" area will be less than 7 and if your goal is to have an improved financial condition, then you can work on "Affirmations for wealth"/ "Affirmations for Job and Money" (as per "List of Affirmations" at pg. 23.

2. **Category 2- "I know my goals, but I don't know my limiting beliefs around them":**

Congratulations to you for having clarity in life! If you have tried hard to achieve that goal or are still trying but have not achieved it so far. Then you just need to understand the limiting beliefs associated with that area. Limit beliefs are negative or self-doubting thoughts and convictions that hold individuals back from reaching their full potential. Once you get the clarity about your limiting beliefs then through affirming a counter positive thought, its effects can be nullified. Reflecting on following questions will help you assess your limiting beliefs in the area of your life that you want to transform:

Area of life	Choose the area which you want to transform and then write 5 most negative statements/ disempowering beliefs about it (that you believe to be true)
Career: Your professional ambitions and goals.	
Finances: Goals related to income, savings, and financial security.	
Health and Fitness: Goals related to physical and mental health.	
Personal Growth: Goals for learning and self-improvement.	
Relationships: Goals for building and maintaining meaningful connections with yourself and others around.	
Spirituality: Goals related to fulfilling your purpose and giving back to the world through your interests and passions.	

Answers to the last column will give you clarity about your limiting beliefs that you want to transform through the power of affirmations. Once you are clear about your limiting beliefs, follow the guidelines given for Category 3.

Always remember that there are no right or wrong limiting beliefs. Each individual can have different limiting beliefs. The aim of this book is to help you identify your limiting beliefs and use them as raw material so that they can be transformed into empowering beliefs. The below examples explain how to use the above questionnaire to get insight about limiting beliefs:

Example-1: If you are not satisfied with your relationship with your boss, then do some introspection and then think about your negative thoughts about this relationship, is it:

    I.   All bosses bully their subordinates.

    II.   Bosses take all the credit.

    III.   Bosses don't share knowledge, etc.

This implies that you have developed a negative belief about the relationship between boss and subordinate. To transform this, you can use these affirmations: "I have a very supportive boss", "My boss is helping me to achieve greater success in my career", etc.

Example-2: If you are not satisfied with your financial situation, then do some soul searching and check your limiting beliefs around money, the most common ones are:

    I.   Money does not grow on trees.

    II.   Money is the root of all evil.

    III.   Money doesn't buy happiness.

    IV.   I'm not good with money, etc.

This implies that you have developed a negative belief about your relationship with wealth and money. To transform this, you can use these affirmations: "money is flowing in my life freely and comfortably" or an affirmation of your choice from "List of Affirmations" at pg. 23.

3. **Category 3- "I know my goals and I know my limiting beliefs around them":**

   Congratulations! You are clear about the area of your life that you want to transform. That means you are halfway through. Now you just have to select the most relevant affirmation that is aligned to your goal from the "List of Affirmations" given at pg. 23 and start affirming in various ways mentioned below, (always remember that *faith, repetition, and consistency* are essential to manifesting affirmations in life):

   1. Write your affirmations in a journal (refer to the 30-Day Challenge given at pg. 65)

   2. Repeat them in your heart as many times as you can.

   3. Speak it aloud to yourself.

   4. Listen to the recorded version of your affirmations.

   5. Write it on a piece of paper or sticky note, place it on your desk, whiteboard, shelf, etc. and see it regularly.

   6. Visualize it in a meditative state.

   7. Use it as your password for different websites/ logins.

   8. Look into the mirror and repeat your affirmations to yourself.

   9. To enhance the power of affirmation, keep affirming: "I release all the resistance to a good life, and the power of affirmation is working in my life."

10. Try to incorporate it in your daily conversations, i.e., whenever talking to others, I repeat these affirmations frequently: "I am awesome", "My life is filled with abundance of goodness", "I am receiving blessings from the universe", etc.

CHAPTER-6
IMPORTANT GUIDELINES FOR
EFFECTIVE AFFIRMATION

1. Be specific: Be clear and specific about what you want to affirm. Instead of general statements like "I am successful," try to create affirmations that are more specific and tailored to your goals or desires. For example, "I am attracting new opportunities that align with my passion and skills." Tailor your affirmations to your specific needs, goals, and desires. Customize them to resonate with who you are and what you want to achieve. This personalization enhances the effectiveness and relevance of the affirmations for you.

2. Use correct language: The affirmations should be phrased in present tense or present continuous tense; this helps the mind believe that they are already true or happening. Affirmations should never be phrased in the future tense. For example, instead of saying "I will be confident," say "I am confident and capable" or "I am becoming confident every day".

3. Use positive language: Frame your affirmations in positive terms, focusing on what you want rather than what you don't want. Instead of saying, "I am no longer afraid," say, "I am courageous and fearlessly winning over my challenges."

4. Use powerful and empowering words: Choose words that are simple, evoke strong emotions, and create a sense of empowerment. For example, replace generalized statements like "I am okay" with "I am resilient, strong, and capable of handling any challenge."

5. Repeat affirmations consistently: Repetition is key to ingraining affirmations into your subconscious mind. Create a daily practice where you repeat your affirmations multiple times, whether verbally, in writing, or through visualization. Consistency is important, so make it a habit to reaffirm your positive statements regularly.

6. Believe in the affirmations: Have faith and believe in the power of your affirmations with purity of intention. The more you truly believe in the statements you are affirming, the stronger their impact will be on your mindset and actions. This will help in transforming reality at a faster pace.

7. Engage your senses and emotions: Make your affirmations more vivid by engaging multiple senses. Visualize yourself living out the affirmations, feel the emotions associated with them, and even incorporate movement or physical actions if it feels natural to you.

Remember, affirmations are a personal practice, and there is no right or wrong way to do them. Experiment with different approaches and techniques to find what works best for you. The most important aspect is to embrace and internalize the positive statements, allowing them to shape your thoughts and beliefs positively.

CHAPTER-7
DON'TS OF AFFIRMATIONS

1. Don't doubt your capabilities: Whatever affirmations you choose, have full faith in them, and do not do them with doubt in your heart. Your life is infinite, and whatever you affirm can be achieved through correct actions.

2. Don't be fearful: Fear creates doubt in our minds and is the biggest block in manifesting affirmations. Be confident while affirming your goals.

3. Don't be desperate: Desperation to achieve any goal can actually delay the realization of the goal. You have to affirm it and let it go: the universe will manifest it at the most appropriate time in your life.

4. Don't use negative language: Avoid using negative language or focusing on what you don't want or fear. Keep your affirmations positively framed, e.g., if you are fearful about public speaking, then don't use this affirmation: "I don't fear public speaking", but replace it with "I am a confident public speaker".

5. Don't rush through affirmations: Take your time with each affirmation and give it your full attention. Sloppy or hurried repetitions may dilute their effectiveness.

6. Don't be in a negative/doubtful mindset: It's important to approach affirmations with an open and positive mindset. If you're feeling skeptical or negative, take a moment to shift your mindset before practicing affirmations.

7. Don't affirm about actions by others: always focus on actions to be taken by you, and don't affirm regarding actions by others. e.g., if you are not getting good grades in a subject, don't affirm that: "My teacher is giving me good grades", instead affirm this: " I know this subject well' '.

8. Don't be impatient for immediate results: Affirmations take time to work effectively. Avoid getting discouraged if you don't see immediate results. Consistency and faith are key.

9. Don't repeat affirmations mechanically: To maximize the impact of affirmations, avoid mindlessly repeating them. Engage your emotions, visualize, and truly believe in the power of each statement.

10. Don't underestimate the power of action: While affirmations can shape your mindset, they need to be backed up by action. Take inspired and aligned actions towards your goals to support the manifestation process.

11. Don't compare yourself to others: Your affirmations should be focused on your own desires, goals, and personal growth. Avoid comparing yourself to others or trying to affirm things solely based on others' achievements or experiences.

By following these guidelines and don'ts, you can ensure that your affirmation practice is effective, empowering, and aligned with your personal growth journey.

Always remember that affirmations are a personal practice, and what works for one person may not work for another. It's important to experiment, customize, and adapt these guidelines to fit your own needs and preferences. Take the time to discover what resonates with you and creates the most positive impact on your mindset and well-being.

CHAPTER-8
LIST OF AFFIRMATIONS

(Compilation of Affirmations related to various areas of life)

Affirmation for Self-love

1. I love the person I see in the mirror.

2. I love myself just as I am today.

3. I choose to be kind to myself.

4. I am my own best friend.

5. It is natural for me to love myself.

6. I am grateful to be the person I am.

7. I love each part of myself.

8. I honor my life.

9. I appreciate all the ways that I am unique.

10. I accept my awesomeness.

11. I love who I am.

12. I am calm and relaxed in all situations.

13. I am relaxed and calm.

14. I am comfortable around other people.

15. I am thankful and grateful for the good in my life.

16. I am releasing all negative emotions from my system.

17. I deserve a peaceful and loving life.

18. I am breathing slowly and deeply, filling myself with calmness.

19. I am letting go of all my worries and fears.

20. I deserve happiness and joy.

21. I am calm and at ease.

22. I surround myself with peace and pleasant emotions.

23. I choose to move my focus on happy experiences.

24. Despite how I feel, I understand this feeling and situation are temporary.

25. Serenity, tranquillity, and other pleasurable emotions engulf my being.

26. All I need is within me now.

27. As my body and mind become more relaxed, I can problem-solve more effectively.

28. I am reclaiming my power.

29. I am naturally stress-free.

30. I am letting go of my worries.

31. I am in control of my life.

32. I am a positive person who attracts positive things into my life.

33. I am equipped to handle this situation effectively.

34. This situation will pass, so I choose to deal with it calmly.

35. I trust my intuition and I am always guided to make wise decisions.

36. My peace is my power.

37. Today, and every day, I choose joy.

"You are enough" Affirmations

1. I am whole, complete, and perfect.

2. I am worthy just as I am.

3. I am enough just as I am.

4. I wholeheartedly believe in myself.

5. I confidently welcome new experiences.

6. I can achieve anything I set my mind to.

7. I know my value and will not lessen or shrink myself for anything or anyone.

8. I am fearless in the pursuit of what sets my soul on fire.

9. I am worthy of respect from myself and others.

10. I am motivated, persistent, and successful.

11. I am pure, positive energy.

12. I hold the key to my own happiness.

13. I love the person I am, both inside and out.

14. I am ready to receive abundance of goodness in my life.

15. I am important and respect worthy.
16. I am worthy of love.

17. I am a unique gift to the world.

Affirmations for Spiritual Awakening

1. I honor the Divine within me.

2. I am connected to my higher divinity.

3. I am open to new ideas.

4. Information I need comes to me easily.

5. The world is my teacher.

6. I am guided by a higher power and inner wisdom.

7. I am worthy of love from divine energy.

8. I am open to letting go of my attachments.

9. I live in the present moment.

10. I am an extension of the Universe, and The Universe is kind and loving.

11. I am connected with the wisdom of the universe.

12. I am a spiritual being in a human body.

13. I honor the sacred divinity that exists within me.

14. I am pure, beautiful, radiant light.

15. My body is a beautiful home for my radiant soul.

16. I am divinely protected, inspired, and guided by the Universe.

17. I am deeply and unconditionally loved by the Universe.

18. I am worthy of unconditional love from divine energy.

19. I am connected to a limitless source of creativity, abundance, health, happiness, and love.

20. I surrender to the loving will of the Universe.

21. I am my highest, most authentic self.

22. My highest self guides my actions and decisions.

23. I am aligned with my soul's purpose and truth.

24. I am always divinely and lovingly guided.

25. I know deep inner peace.

26. Eternal peace flows to and through me.

27. I release the need to control my life and surrender to a higher power.

28. I trust my intuition and listen to the wisdom of the universe.

29. I am loved, cherished, and adored by this Universe.

30. Pure white light flows through me and heals my body, mind, and spirit.

31. I am aligned with the highest frequency of love.

32. I am clear about what I want and take inspired action to achieve my dreams.

33. I release doubt and welcome faith.

34. Every day, I feel more connected to my soul.

35. I openly accept spiritual guidance from a higher power.

36. I bravely let go and allow the Universe to reveal its beautiful plan for me.

37. I trust that the Universe gives me exactly what I need at exactly the right time.

38. I am eternally connected to the divine source of the Universe.

39. Even when the world is immersed in darkness, I walk forward in faith, love, and light.

40. The light and energy of the Universe flow within me.

41. I have unshakeable faith in my divine path.

42. I'm Source Energy in the human body, and I can do anything.

43. I surrender to my highest good.

44. I surrender to the highest good for all.

45. I am love, I am light, I am connected to all.

46. I am on my perfect path for my life purpose.

47. I become more enlightened each day.

48. I am in harmony with nature and animals.

49. Everything is connected. I am connected to all of life.

50. My life is beautiful and sacred.

51. My soul is always guiding me.

52. I easily recognize divine wisdom as it flows to me.

53. My life flows beautifully, and I am always learning from my experiences.

54. I'm learning to release attachments to physical things, my happiness comes from within.

55. I observe my challenges with curiosity about what they can teach me.

56. I am a divine being.

57. I enjoy the little things in life.

58. My soul chose this life experience for growth and

expansion.

59. I am a cooperative component with the universe, on the leading edge of creation.

60. Death is nothing to be afraid of because I am more than my physical body.

61. I am open to knowing myself more deeply.

62. Separation is an illusion; I am connected to all that is.

63. I am joyful.

64. I trust the universe and know that I am always safe.

65. I am healing on all levels of my being.

66. I understand that I am an important connection in the web of life.

67. I am more than my ego-self.

68. I vibrate at the frequency of appreciation and pure joy.

69. My crown chakra is open and in perfect balance.

70. I choose to live in the present moment because 'now' is all there is. All of my power is in the now.

71. I know that everyone is at a different level of spiritual awareness, and doing the best they can.

72. I release limiting thoughts, beliefs, and relationships that no longer serve me.

73. Abundance is a natural result of my gratitude and appreciation for life.

74. Prosperity flows to me with ease when I'm in alignment with my true self.

75. I am oneness.

76. I am healed on all levels of my being.

77. I am fully aware and awake.

78. I feel a strong spiritual connection to my higher self.

79. I have unlimited possibilities available to me.

80. I am connected to the universe.

81. All is well.

82. Everything I seek is within me.

83. I accept and receive divine energy to flow throughout my Chakras.

84. I am divinely guided.

85. I receive blessings from the Universe.

86. My experiences are blissful.

87. I am in complete control of my emotions.

88. I am optimistic and confident.

89. I am aware of my inner beauty.

90. I embrace life and cherish my spirit.

91. I radiate love and warmth.

92. I respect the intentions and emotions of others.

93. I am open to receiving new energy.

94. I surrender to the infinite power of the Universe.

Affirmations for Positive thinking

1. I accept myself for who I am.

2. I am building my future.

3. I choose to think positively every moment.

4. My happiness is up to me.

5. I start my day with a positive mindset.

6. Anything is possible.

7. I radiate positive energy.

8. Wonderful things are going to happen to me.

9. I can take deep breaths.

10. With every breath, I feel stronger.

11. I only compare myself to myself.

12. I strive everyday to become a better version of myself.

13. I can do anything.

14. It is enough to do my best.

15. My body is a vessel of wellness.

16. Today I am focusing on what makes me feel good.

17. I feel my emotions and I have the power to change them.

18. I feel proud of being myself.

Affirmations for Relationships

1. I am letting love into my life.

1. I feel surrounded by love everywhere.

2. I receive love in abundance from everyone I meet.

3. I am grateful for all the love and affection I get.

4. I deserve fulfilling relationships.

5. My heart is open.

6. I am attracting trusting and loving relationships.

7. Real love starts with me.

8. I see love everywhere I go.

9. I am grateful for the people who love me.

10. I am worthy of the compliments I receive.

11. I am worthy of love and care.

12. I deserve the love I receive.

13. I love myself and am open to love.

14. The more love I give, the more I receive.

15. I love to give and receive love.

16. I deserve real and authentic love.

17. I am open and ready to find true love.

18. I believe in love.

19. I am a patient lover.

20. I release my past and am ready to find love.

21. I deserve love as I am.

22. My love is precious.

23. I am meant to have a lifelong love.

24. Love is my priority.

25. I am at peace, knowing love comes naturally to me.

26. I am unique, interesting, and intelligent.

27. I spread love, and it returns to me.

28. I am open to love in all forms.

29. The universe is guiding me to love.

30. I am fulfilled.

31. I make time for those I love.

32. The love I seek also seeks me.

Affirmations for Marriage

1. I value the commitment we have made to each other and honor our vows.

2. I feel safe and secure in my marriage and know I am loved.

3. I communicate openly with my husband/wife and speak with honesty and truth.

4. I show my husband/wife lots of love and affection.

5. I am grateful for the love in my life right now.

6. I enjoy spending time with my husband/wife because he/she is my best friend.

7. I am devoted to my spouse.

8. My marriage is divinely protected.

9. With each passing day, my love for my spouse grows stronger.

10. I am thankful for my spouse daily.

11. My spouse and I decide daily to love each other.

12. I believe in my marriage.

13. I am a supportive, loving spouse.

14. I always look for ways that I can contribute to my spouse's happiness.

15. My spouse is and will always be my best friend.

16. Wonderful things are in store for us, my spouse and me.

17. My marriage is the most sacred thing to me.

18. I am enjoying the things in my marriage that I already have.

19. I love my spouse unconditionally.

20. Our marriage is growing stronger every day.

21. our love, care and respect for each is growing every day.

Affirmations for Friends

1. I feel safe with my friends.

2. My friends make me laugh.

3. My best friend makes the best company.

4. All my friends are lovely people in their own way.

5. My friends and I encourage one another in all our efforts.

6. I express how much I care for my friends.

7. I am a reliable friend.

8. I always listen to my friends with empathy.

9. I am a great listener.

10. I feel happy with my friends.

11. I am blessed with understanding and supportive friends.

12. I attract amazing friends.

13. I maintain long-lasting friendships.

14. I am a loyal friend.

15. I am an honest friend.

16. I share a deep, loving connection with my friends.

17. I know that I can rely on my friends.

18. Lasting friendships come with ease for me.

19. New friendships are exciting to me.

20. I have the right to choose friends that are healthy for me.

Affirmations for Family

1. My relationship with my family is strong and built on trust and love.

2. I am grateful for all the members of my family.

3. I love my family and they love me.

4. My family deserves happiness.

5. We build each other up.

6. We celebrate each other's happiness and successes.

7. Our state of joy inspires our families to be happy as well.

8. I like spending time with my family.

9. I share a healthy relationship with each member of my family. I enjoy being with my family.

10. My family is my support system.

11. I feel understood by my family.

12. I feel loved by my family.

13. My family supports my passion.

14. I am grateful for my family.

15. It is easy for me to be myself with my family.

16. I love my family unconditionally.

17. I feel grateful to be a part of such a beautiful family.

18. I listen to my family's needs.

19. I always look to understand my family.

Affirmations for Health

1. My body feels good, and I radiate good feelings.

2. Every day is a new day full of hope, happiness, and health.

3. I am always happy, hale, and hearty.

4. I am vigorous, energetic, and full of vitality.

5. Every passing day my body is becoming more energetic, healthier.

6. I am treating my body as a temple.

7. I love my body for everything amazing it can do!

8. I am at peace with my body, heart, mind, and soul.

9. I lovingly do everything I can to assist my body in maintaining perfect health.

10. I am my greatest well-wisher.

11. I am thriving in my healing journey.

12. Every day is a new day full of hope, happiness, and health.

13. I am always happy, hale, and hearty.

14. I am vigorous, energetic, and full of vitality.

15. I am using my body's innate healing powers to heal my pains.

16. I am full of life force and vitality.

17. My muscles are relaxed.

18. I am enjoying abundance of health, energy, and high life force everyday.

Affirmations for Mental Health

1. I am now in control.

2. Tension in my mind and body is melting away.

3. My mind and body are calm.

4. Calmness washes over me with every deep breath I take.

5. I am feeling better.

6. All is well in my world.

7. I will get through today.

8. I welcome a sense of calm into my life.

9. I give myself permission to feel this way without judgment.

10. It's okay. Everything will be fine.

11. I am brave.

12. I trust the world will help me live my best life.

13. I release tension whenever I exhale.

14. My thoughts are slowing down.

15. I am strong and ready for change.

16. I am freeing myself from stress.

17. I am feeling freer and healthier.

18. I feel calm and peaceful inside.

19. I am more than my thoughts.

20. I choose peace.

21. Letting go of worry is becoming easy.

22. I release all tension in my body.

23. Only good things happen to me.

24. I am balanced.

25. I see the good in myself.

26. I appreciate the goodness in my life.

27. I find more and more to be grateful for.

28. I am proud of myself for making it so far.

29. I am resilient.

30. I value myself.

31. Every day is a gift.

32. I am blessed as life is happening for me.

33. I am loved and appreciated even when it seems like I'm not.

Affirmations to Calm down quickly

1. I am safe and in control.

2. I have done this before, and I can do it again.

3. This too shall pass.

4. I am strong.

5. I trust myself.

6. I am capable.

7. I take things one day at a time.

8. I inhale peace and exhale worry.

9. This feeling is only temporary.

10. I am loved and accepted.

Affirmations for Anxiety Relief

1. I am enough.

2. Look at me go! I can do it all.

3. I love myself.

4. I forgive myself.

5. I let go and I am free.

6. I am doing the best I can and that is enough.

7. I release the past and embrace the present.

8. Wherever I go, I am well.

9. I can handle whatever comes my way.

10. I am safe and protected.

11. I am safe.

12. I am brave.

13. I can move past this moment.

14. I am in charge.

15. As I breathe, I am calm and relaxed.

16. I have survived my anxiety before. I will survive it now.

17. My body is my ally.

18. I inhale white light of peace & positivity.

Affirmations for Social Anxiety

1. I act with confidence because I know what I am doing.

2. I am different and unique, and that is OK.

3. I am safe in the company of others.

4. I love, and I am loved.

5. I am prepared and ready for this situation.

6. People assume I can do this, I know I can, and I will.

7. I like myself and that is enough.

8. I am at ease when talking to other people.

Affirmations for Performance Anxiety

1. I enjoy doing this.

2. I am good at everything I do.

3. Day by day, minute to minute.

4. I am capable and prepared.

5. I let go of control and focus on joy.

6. I am here, I am now, and I am well.

7. I can handle anything that's to come.

8. I am safe in the here and now.

9. I will handle whatever happens like I always do.

10. I choose to see the beauty in my surroundings.

11. I have time to prepare and decide.

Affirmations for Strength and Confidence

1. My mind is a friend to my body.

2. I let go of negative self-talk.

3. I love the body I was born with.

4. I am a special person.

5. I have a loving relationship with my body.

6. I embrace every bit of my body.

7. I love myself unconditionally.

8. I have the power to create the life I want.

9. I can overcome any obstacle.

10. I am worthy of true love.

11. I feel happy.

12. I feel peaceful.

13. I treat my body with care and love.

14. I treat myself with kindness.

15. I am strong and healthy.

16. I am confident.

Affirmations for Courage

1. I can overcome my fears.

2. I can persevere and stay strong.

3. I am free from anxiety.

4. I can overcome any stressful situation.

5. I can make it happen.

6. I'm loved. I'm important. I'm unique.

7. I am supported.

8. I can feel the shift towards peace.

9. I know I am worthy of peace.

10. The peace that I need is inside me.

11. Nobody can help me achieve peace but me.

12. The power is in my hands.

13. I know that problems are temporary.

14. All problems have solutions.

15. I am capable of handling every challenge in my life.

Affirmations for Money Manifestation

1. I know anyone can be wealthy, including me.

2. I love money and money loves me.

3. I accept and receive unexpected money.

4. I am open and receptive to all the wealth life offers me.

5. I embrace new avenues of income.

6. I welcome an unlimited source of income and wealth in my life.

7. I release all negative energy over money.

8. Every day, I choose money and wealth.

9. All the money I have brings me joy.

10. I am worthy of a wealthy life.

11. I love my abundant and positive life.

12. The more I give, the more I receive.

13. I thank the Universe for the money that flows to me.

14. I radiate prosperity, money, and wealth.
15. If others can be wealthy, so can I.

16. Today, no matter where I am, I focus on what I want to see.

17. All the resources I need are within me.

18. I am abundant, rich, wealthy, deserving, worthy.

19. I love my life and everything it provides me with.

20. Abundance is all around me, in everything I do.

21. My finances improve beyond my dreams.

22. Money helps me experience freedom.

23. Money and I can co-exist in harmony.

24. Money is my friend.

25. I attract large sums of money into my life.

26. There are no limits to what I can and will achieve.

27. I am worthy of the wealth I desire.

28. I am financially free.

29. I am grateful for the money I have.

30. I am a money magnet.

31. Wealth and abundance flow to me.

32. I am open to receiving money in my life.

33. I attract money easily and effortlessly.

34. I am worthy of financial success.

35. I am an excellent money manager.

36. I spend money only on things I love.

37. I am generous with my money.

38. I am a great giver and an excellent receiver.

39. Money is drawn to me.

40. I deserve to make more money.

41. I think about money positively.

42. Money is openly flowing into my life.

43. I release all blocks and allow wealth to flow in.

44. I attract money happily in my life.

45. My income is rising at a rapid rate.

46. I always have enough money.

47. Money is abundant to me.

48. I attract money easily and effortlessly.

49. I believe there is enough money for everyone.

50. I am the master of my wealth.

51. I can handle large sums of money.

52. Money creates a positive impact on my life and the life of others.

53. I am at peace with having a lot of money.

54. I can handle massive success with ease.

55. I change the world with my money.

56. I get rich doing what I love.

57. The Universe will always serve my best interests.

58. I am grateful for all the money I have now.

59. I have a positive money mindset.

60. Attracting money comes easily to me.

61. My capacity to hold and grow money expands every day.

62. I release all resistance to attracting money.

63. I am grateful that I can contribute my money to the economy.

64. I am debt-free because money is constantly flowing into my life.

65. The more I focus on joy, the more money I will make.

66. Money flows to me in expected and unexpected ways.

67. My finances improve beyond anything I could ever imagine.

68. I have the power to attract wealth and money into my life.

Affirmations for Wealth

1. I am the master of my wealth.

2. I can handle large amounts of wealth.

3. I am at peace with having prosperity in my life.

4. I can handle massive success with grace.

5. Wealth expands my life's opportunities and experiences.

6. Abundance of wealth creates a positive impact in my life.

7. I am worthy of financial abundance.

8. It is safe for me to be wealthy.

9. My income exceeds my expectations.

10. I can confidently handle large amounts of money.
11. There's plenty more wealth in the world for me.

12. There is wealth all around me to claim.

13. I am creating an abundant future for myself and my family.

14. It is safe for me to be the breadwinner.

15. I am tapped into the universal supply of wealth & luxury.

16. It is safe for me to earn more money than I need.

17. It is safe for me to have savings.

18. I achieve my financial goals with ease.

19. It is safe for me to be financially secure.

20. I have total control of my money.

21. I am worthy of making more money than ever before.

22. It is safe for me to earn more money than anyone I know.

23. I have everything I need to be successful.

24. I am in control of my financial life.

25. I am worthy of great wealth.

26. It is safe for me to enjoy wealth & luxury.

27. Abundance of wealth in life allows me to freely live a life I love.

Affirmations for Students

1. I have a sharp mind which makes me a very good student.

2. My mind's ability to learn and remember is increasing every day.

3. I have a winner's mindset and I love accomplishing my goals.

4. I am advancing to new levels by learning more each day.

5. I feel thankful to be a student and it shows.

6. I radiate positive energy.

7. I am a gifted student, and I can achieve anything.

8. I am a talented and prominent student.

9. I have self-respect and dignity.

10. I make a positive impact on other students' lives.

11. I am kind and courteous to all people.

12. I love my student life!

13. I strive to do my best every day.

14. I embrace life as a student.

15. I am on the journey of becoming a very successful student.

16. I am advancing to new levels by learning more each day.

17. It is possible for me to achieve all my goals because my true potential is limitless.

18. My mind absorbs and processes new information with greater speed.

19. I love gaining knowledge which helps me in growing to my full potential.

20. I have a sharp mind that makes me a very good student.

21. I am a very quick learner.

22. I am very good at gaining knowledge and making proper use of it.

23. My mind's ability to learn and remember is increasing every day.

24. It's okay not to know everything. I can always learn.

25. I start with a positive mindset.

26. I am capable.

27. I am in control of my progress.

28. I create a healthy balance in my life.

29. I can get through everything.

30. I am building my future.

31. I can change the world.

32. I will win at what I put my mind to.

33. I am excited to step into a new world.

34. Anything is possible.

35. I will continue to expand my mind.

36. I am worthy to receive accolades for my performance.

37. Nothing can stop me from living the life of my dreams.

38. I am a beautiful person. I matter. I am strong. I am genuine. I can do anything I put my mind to. I've got this.

39. I choose healthy ways to deal with stress.

40. There is no reason for me to compare myself to others.

41. I'm only human and we all make mistakes.

42. Success is not final, and failure is not fatal. It's the courage to persevere that counts in the end.

43. I am blessed to live this life that I have created.

44. Every day, I improve myself in some way.

45. I am worthy of deep connections.

46. I always stay focused on my studies.

47. I concentrate all my efforts on the things I want to accomplish.

48. I focus on the important tasks first.

49. I focus on one task at a time.

50. My ability to focus is increasing which is making me a peak performer.

51. I always stay focused on my studies.

52. I am recognized as a student with immense focus and determination.

53. I am truly attentive to my work.

54. Every day in every way I am becoming more focused on what I do.

55. Staying focused now comes naturally to me.

56. Focusing comes naturally to me.

57. I always stay focused on my studies.

58. I always enjoy my studies.

59. I stay focused while studying for exams.

60. I focus well to get good grades.

61. When I am exposed to information that benefits me, I absorb it like a sponge!

62. I will focus on the important things, and let the rest go.

63. My time is valuable.

64. I am free of distractions.

65. Studying with focus comes easily and naturally to me.

Affirmations for Excelling Exams

1. I am always relaxed during exams.

2. Getting good grades is natural for me.

3. I am learning to enjoy studying.

4. While writing answers, I recall information quickly.

5. I work both hard and smartly to clear my exams.

6. I look forward to a great result of my exams.

7. I succeed even in stressful situations.

8. Recalling information while writing in exams is easy.

9. I am good at turning my nervous feelings into high confidence.

10. I will do well in this exam as I am well prepared.

11. I am an excellent student.

12. I always pass exams with flying colors.

13. I know what I need to know for this exam.

14. I feel good about myself and my preparations for tests and

exams.

15. I will pass my exams.

Affirmations for Valuing Education

1. Education is the gateway to my future! Today I make the most of my academic opportunities.

2. Today I take charge of my education. The more I learn, the more I achieve.

3. I value my education as it prepares me for a bright future.

4. Learning is life. I love learning and I am good at it!

5. I respect my education because it creates a more complete me.

6. I am always open to learning in a better way.

7. Today I set aside my fears and achieve all my educational goals.

8. Whatever I need to learn always comes my way at just the right moment.

9. I chose to move forward every day, growing and learning as I go!

10. As my demand for my learning grows, my learning expands.

11. I am a talented student, and I am going to learn a lot today.

12. I will follow my dreams.

13. My self-worth is not determined by any number on a scale.

14. I am confident that I can solve life's problems successfully.

Affirmations for Manifesting New Job

1. I am ready for a new job.

2. I deserve a wonderful new job.

3. I am happy and positive at my new job.

4. I am so excited about my new job.

5. I'm ready to elevate my life with a new job.

6. I'm so thankful to have a job with a positive work environment.

7. It is easy and exciting to search for a new job.

8. I thank the Universe for helping me secure this job.

9. I am happy and content in my new job.

10. There is an abundance of amazing jobs out there that would be perfect for me.

11. It's easy for me to find a job that I love.

12. I am attracting the best and most suitable job for me right now.

13. The Universe is helping my new job to manifest with ease.

14. I'm always attracting better and better jobs.

15. The Universe supports me in this career change.

16. Good job offers are flowing to me effortlessly.

17. My positive attitude is opening new doors for me.

18. I deserve a good job, and I am getting it.

19. I am natural at job interviews.

20. I find it easy to connect with employers.

21. Job opportunities fall right into my lap.

22. I am open and receptive to all job opportunities.

23. I confidently demonstrate my strengths at job interviews.

24. I feel prepared to ace this job interview.

25. I am the best person for this job and the interviewers see that.

26. I'm so excited to receive the perfect job offer.

27. I am valuable, and employers see that.

28. I deserve to get this job.

29. I feel at ease during job interviews.

30. My energy is contagious – job interviews are easy for me.

31. I am the perfect candidate for this position.

Affirmations to Manifest Dream Job

1. The Universe is bringing me the best job for me.

2. I am working at my dream job and enjoying every minute.

3. I am attracting my dream job to me.

4. My perfect job is manifesting for me.

5. I am worthy of doing a job that I love.

6. The Universe is leading me to my dream job.

7. I am worthy of getting my dream job.

8. The perfect job for me is out there and I'm ready to find it.

9. I'm perfectly qualified for my dream job.

10. I am in alignment with my dream job.

11. I feel excited to go to work each day.

12. I love having a job with flexible hours that works with my schedule.

13. My work feels satisfying and rewarding.

14. I have the knowledge and skills essential for my dream job.

15. I landed my dream job, and I am so grateful.

16. I love what I do for work.

17. Every day my energy aligns even more with my ideal job.

18. I am being divinely guided towards my perfect job.

19. I release all negative thoughts and beliefs getting in the way of my dream job.

Affirmations for Job Satisfaction & Money

1. I have a satisfying job with a wonderful pay.

2. Life sends me money-making, joy-inducing opportunities every day.

3. My employers love paying me generously for my work.

4. I love getting paid for work I enjoy.

5. I'm worthy of respect and fair compensation for my work.

6. I am rewarded abundantly for the work I do.

7. My new job brings me freedom, fun and financial

abundance.

8. I'm breaking through to my next level of career and financial success.

9. I am richly rewarded for the work I do.

10. I am an energetic match for my dream job and salary

11. My salary potential is unlimited.

12. I am financially stable and secure because of my work.

13. The work I do pays me generously.

14. The work I put out into the world brings me a great financial return.

15. My salary is always growing.

16. People love to pay me for my skills.

Affirmations for Successful Career

1. I am a magnet for new career opportunities.

2. I am a magnet for a successful career.

3. I find it easy to network with others.

4. I release my limiting beliefs over my career.

5. There are so many great career opportunities available for me.

6. Doors of new opportunity are always opening for me.

7. I am confident about my worth, skills, and knowledge.

8. I trust the Universe to lead me to the perfect career.

9. I deserve to work at an amazing company that values me.

10. I'm so thankful my boss recognizes my hard work and rewards me for it.

11. I'm surrounded with the best people at work.

12. I am open to opportunities for advancement.

13. I have unique gifts and talents that are an asset to my career.

14. Everyone at work appreciates me.

15. I am where I want to be; I am on the right career path.

16. I am ambitious and inspired to achieve my career goals.

17. I deserve to move ahead in my career.

18. I'm ready to attract my next level of career success.

Affirmations for Successful Business

1. I am a magnet for new Business opportunities.

2. I am a magnet for clients.

3. My business is growing every day.

4. I am ready to receive exponential growth in my business.

5. My growing business is helping all my stakeholders.

6. I find it easy to network with others.

7. I release my limiting beliefs over my successful business.

8. I am attracting all business opportunities from the Universe.

9. My clients always support my business ideas.

10. Doors of new opportunities are always opening for me.

11. I am confident in my worth, skills, and knowledge.

12. I trust the Universe to lead me to the perfect growth plan.

13. I deserve to create an amazing work environment at my business.

14. I'm so thankful to all my employees for their hard work, dedication & sincerity.

15. I'm surrounded by the best people at work.

16. I am open to opportunities for advancement.

17. I have unique gifts and talents that are an asset to my growth.

18. Everyone at work appreciates me.

19. I am where I want to be; I am on the right growth path.

20. I create abundance of wealth through my business for myself & others.

21. I am ambitious and inspired to achieve my business goals.

22. I have all the energy, time & knowledge to grow my business for the benefit of all.

30-DAY AFFIRMATION CHALLENGE

Time to take some transformative actions. Let's work on it one by one. Pick one area of life and choose your five favorite affirmations related to this area from the above list. Write it every day for the next 30 days and see the transformation in your life.

Example: If you pick the first five affirmations for Self-love, write them like:

1. I love myself just as I am today.

2. I am a special person.

3. I see the good in myself.

4. I am my own best friend.

5. I accept my awesomeness.

Repeat these affirmations for the next 30 days by writing them daily, repeating them in your heart like a chant, and saying them aloud in front of the mirror at least once a day. And be ready to receive positive transformations in your life. Once this worksheet is over, you can repeat this whole process in any diary/notebook/ journal. Always remember that faith, repetition, discipline, and consistency are the keys to faster manifestations. Don't wait anymore and start it today itself!

Meanwhile, I am praying for your life to be filled with love, hope, courage, and positive energy!

worksheet   for 30-Day affirmation challenge

Day-1   Date: _____

1._____

2._____

3._____

4._____

5._____

Day-2   Date: _____

1._____

2._____

3._____

4._____

5._____

Day-3   Date: _____

1._____

2._____

3._____

4._____

5._____

Day-4   Date: _____

1._____

2._____

3._____

4._____

5._____

Day-5   Date: _____

1._____

2._____

3._____

4._____

5._____

Day-6   Date: _____

1._____

2._____

3._____

4._____

5._____

Day-7   Date: _____

1._____

2._____

3._____

4._____

5._____

Day-8   Date: _____

1._____

2._____

3._____

4._____

5._____

Day-9   Date: _____

1._____

2._____

3._____

4._____

5._____

Day-10   Date: _____

1._____

2._____

3._____

4._____

5._____

Day-11   Date: _____

1._____

2._____

3._____

4._____

5._____

Day-12   Date: _____

1._____

2._____

3._____

4._____

5._____

Day-13   Date: _____

1. _____
2. _____
3. _____
4. _____
5. _____

Day-14   Date: _____

1. _____
2. _____
3. _____
4. _____
5. _____

Day-15   Date: _____

1. _____
2. _____
3. _____
4. _____
5. _____

Day-16   Date: _____

1._____

2._____

3._____

4._____

5._____

Day-17   Date: _____

1._____

2._____

3._____

4._____

5._____

Day-18   Date: _____

1._____

2._____

3._____

4._____

5._____

Day-19   Date: _____

1._____

2._____

3._____

4._____

5._____

Day-20   Date: _____

1._____

2._____

3._____

4._____

5._____

Day-21   Date: _____

1._____

2._____

3._____

4._____

5._____

Day-22   Date: _____

1._____

2._____

3._____

4._____

5._____

Day-23   Date: _____

1._____

2._____

3._____

4._____

5._____

Day-24   Date: _____

1._____

2._____

3._____

4._____

5._____

Day-25   Date: _____

1._____

2._____

3._____

4._____

5._____

Day-26   Date: _____

1._____

2._____

3._____

4._____

5._____

Day-27   Date: _____

1._____

2._____

3._____

4._____

5._____

Day-28   Date: _____

1._____

2._____

3._____

4._____

5._____

Day-29   Date: _____

1._____

2._____

3._____

4._____

5._____

Day-30   Date: _____

1._____

2._____

3._____

4._____

5._____

FAQS RELATED TO AFFIRMATIONS

Question-1: Can I do affirmation in any language?

Answer: You can do affirmations in any language that you feel comfortable with and that has personal meaning to you. So, whether it's your native language or another language you are proficient in, feel free to use the language that feels right for you when practicing affirmations. The key is to make the affirmations personal, meaningful, and aligned to your goals and desires.

The effectiveness of affirmations depends on your beliefs and emotional connection to the words or phrases you're using. If a particular language resonates with you or has cultural or personal significance, it can make your affirmations more powerful and meaningful.

Question-2: Can I use the power of affirmations to achieve results in others' lives?

Answer: Affirmation is a personal practice for transforming your life through reprogramming your own subconscious mind through the right choice of words. Conceptually, affirming to change others' lives may not work that effectively, as it is not directly going through their subconscious mind. Therefore, it is always advisable for an individual to do their own affirmations. However, affirmations can be done for the effect of the change in your life. For example, if a mother wants her rude child to behave nicely, she can affirm with full faith, "I am grateful that my child is courteous and polite". Instead of trying to change others directly through affirmations, focus on being a positive and supportive presence in their lives and encourage them to make their own choices.

Question-3: At what age should I start doing affirmations?

Answer: You can start unleashing the power of affirmation as young as the age of three. It can be used as soon as you start understanding the language and when you can feel the emotions attached to those words. Affirmations can be helpful for people of all ages, including children and teenagers.

Question-4: How much time needs to be dedicated for affirmations?

Answer: The amount of time you dedicate to affirmations can vary depending on your personal preferences, goals, and schedule. It's more important to focus on the quality and sincerity of your affirmations than the quantity. Repeating a few powerful affirmations with genuine belief can be more effective than rushing through a long list of them. Whether you spend a few minutes or longer each day on affirmations, consistency and faith are the most important factors in their effectiveness. Authenticity is key to making affirmations work.

Question-5: What if I am unable to do it daily?

Answer: Consistency is the key to effective manifesting through affirmation. Affirmations are like building up your mental muscles, so the process is like developing your physical muscles. Just as you engage in physical exercise on a regular basis to strengthen your muscles, it is important to maintain discipline by doing affirmations on a daily basis. Intermittently practicing affirmations can create openings for negative thoughts to infiltrate, potentially causing a delay in the manifestation process.

Question-6: How much time is required to get the results of affirmations?

Answer: The time required to get results from affirmations can vary widely from person to person and depend on several factors, including beliefs and mindset, consistency, specific goals, emotional attachment, patience, etc. Results can be gradual, and it's essential to trust the process and be patient. Some people may start seeing changes in a few weeks, while for others, it might take several months. The key is to stay consistent and maintain a positive attitude as you work toward your goals through affirmations. You can compare your affirmation to the order that you have placed in the restaurant of the universe and then wait patiently for it to be served. While waiting for our order in a restaurant, we just enjoy the music and ambience without getting worried about what dishes are being served to others or when our order will be served. Similarly, when we don't attach the energy of worry to our affirmation, it manifests just at the right time in our lives.

Question-7: What should I do if I don't get the results of my affirmations?

Answer: If you're not getting the results you desire from your affirmations, it's important to review and adjust your approach. Check if your affirmations are drafted for specific outcomes, use positive language in the present or present continuous tense, practice with faith supported by emotional engagement, do it consistently, and back it with the right actions in alignment with the affirmations. Affirmations can be a powerful tool for self-improvement and mindset change, but their effectiveness increases when used in conjunction with other positive habits and practices.

Question-8: Is there a minimum number of days for which I should do a particular manifestation?

Answer: There is no universally agreed-upon minimum or maximum number of days one should engage in affirmations. Affirmations involve setting the right intentions with faith in the power that lies in our lives to achieve the desired goal. In my opinion, the minimum number of days for an affirmation is 30 days. The maximum number of days depends on your perseverance and belief in that affirmation to manifest.

Question-9: Can I use future tense language in my affirmations?

Answer: Tomorrow never comes, so any affirmation done in future tense puts it in a timeline that is yet to happen. whereas when we use present/ present continuous tense language, it sends a signal of achieving the deceased goal and thus evokes positive emotions associated with the achievement. Our subconscious mind cannot differentiate between physical reality and perceived reality. It is recommended to use the present tense/ Present continuous tense to make your affirmations more immediate and believable. For example, say "I am courageous" rather than "I will be courageous."

Question-10: Can I create my own affirmations?

Answer: Yes, creating your own affirmations tailored to your specific goals and desires is highly encouraged. Personalized affirmations tend to have a more significant impact because they resonate with you on a deeper level.

Question-11: What if I don't believe the affirmations I'm making?

Answer: It's common for people to initially have doubts or resistance when starting with affirmations. If you don't fully believe them, start with statements that are easy to believe and feel more attainable, and gradually work your way up to more ambitious affirmations. Through perseverance, bit by bit, your faith will be developed, and then you will start reaping all the benefits of this power of affirmations.

Question-12: Can affirmations replace therapy or professional help?

Answer: Affirmations can be a valuable tool for personal growth and well-being, but they should not replace professional help when needed. If you're dealing with serious issues, it's essential to seek guidance from a qualified therapist or counselor.

Question-13: Can anyone use affirmations?

Answer: Yes, anyone who is willing to take transformative actions to build a better life can use affirmations. Anyone who uses this tool should do it with some level of faith in it.

Question-14: Can affirmations help with overcoming negative thoughts and self-doubt?

Answer: Yes, affirmations are often used to counteract negative thinking patterns and self-doubt. By replacing negative thoughts with positive affirmations, you can gradually shift your mindset from "victim" to "Victor".

Question-15: Do affirmations guarantee success?

Answer: Affirmations are a tool to support personal growth and change, but they are not a guarantee of success. They work best when combined with action, sincere efforts, and a positive mindset.

Question-16: Can affirmations be used for specific goals, like weight loss or career success?

Answer: Yes, affirmations can be customized for specific goals. For example, you can create affirmations related to healthy eating habits or career advancement to help you stay focused and motivated.

Remember that the effectiveness of affirmations can vary from person to person, so it's important to approach them with an open mind and consistency to see which one works for you the most.

While affirmations are a powerful and valuable tool, they are not a magic solution and should be part of a holistic approach to personal growth and self-improvement. The magic lies in your life, and affirmations help you to bring the best out of it.

BOOK RECOMMENDATIONS

i. Power of subconscious mind -Dr. Joseph Murphy.

ii. Mind power - John Kehoe

iii. You can heal your life- Louise L Hay

iv. The Power of Positive Thinking - Norman Vincent Peale.

v. Secret- Rhonda Byrne

SYNOPSIS

"Everything About Affirmations" is a comprehensive resource for anyone seeking to tap into the infinite potential existing in their own life. It provides techniques for creating and utilizing affirmations, offering customized options for various aspects of life. The book also includes a 30-Day Affirmation Challenge worksheet and answers to common questions. The book is a comprehensive resource for anyone seeking to tap into their infinite potential and unlock the transformative power of their thoughts and beliefs. This book equips the reader with the knowledge and tools to unlock the transformative power of their own thoughts and beliefs so that they can achieve abundance of goodness in all areas of their life. The mission of this book is to empower readers with the hope and courage required to live life to its fullest and "Claim The Universe" by unleashing the power within.

ABOUT THE AUTHOR

 Mandvi Gupta, an electrical engineer, discovered the power of the subconscious mind while working in the corporate world. She researched various concepts of Mind Power techniques and experienced significant transformations in her own life. This passion led her to focus on mentoring and coaching others in Mind Power techniques. She has become certified as a Professional Life Coach, NLP practitioner, DMIT analyst, Mid Brain Activation facilitator, EFT practitioner, and Ho'oponopono therapist. These certifications equipped her with a comprehensive skill set to guide individuals in harnessing the power of their minds.

Mandvi believes in everyone's infinite innate potential to live a life filled with contentment, joy, and success. She aims to empower individuals to break free from limiting beliefs and create the life they truly desire. Through personalized coaching sessions, workshops, and online programs, she assists individuals in developing a deeper understanding of their subconscious mind and its impact on their thoughts, emotions, and actions.

In conclusion, her journey from engineering to mentoring and coaching in Mind Power techniques has been a natural progression fueled by a desire to help individuals by unleashing their infinite mind power. She is dedicated to continuing her own personal growth and learning while also empowering individuals to break free from their limiting beliefs and create extraordinary lives for themselves.

Manufactured by Amazon.ca
Bolton, ON

38981763R00052